P9-DDG-012

DINOSAUR BONE WAR

Cope and Marsh's Fossil Feud

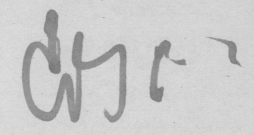

DINOSAUR
BONE WAR
Cope and Marsh's Fossil Feud

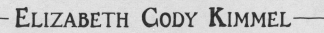

ELIZABETH CODY KIMMEL

Landmark Books®

Random House 🏠 New York

*Special thanks to Dr. Robert T. Bakker for his
assistance in the preparation of this book.*

Text copyright © 2006 by Elizabeth Cody Kimmel

All rights reserved.
Published in the United States by Random House Children's Books,
a division of Random House, Inc., New York.

RANDOM HOUSE and colophon and LANDMARK BOOKS and colophon
are registered trademarks of Random House, Inc.

www.randomhouse.com/kids

Educators and librarians, for a variety of teaching tools,
visit us at www.randomhouse.com/teachers

Library of Congress Cataloging-in-Publication Data
Kimmel, Elizabeth Cody.
Dinosaur bone war : Cope and Marsh's fossil feud /
Elizabeth Cody Kimmel. — 1st ed.
p. cm.
ISBN-13: 978-0-375-81349-8 (pbk.) — ISBN-13: 978-0-375-91349-5 (lib. bdg.)
ISBN-10: 0-375-81349-7 (pbk.) — ISBN-10: 0-375-91349-1 (lib. bdg.)
1. Cope, E. D. (Edward Drinker), 1840–1897. 2. Marsh, Othniel Charles,
1831–1899. 3. Paleontologists—United States—Biography.
4. Fossils—Collection and preservation—West (U.S.)—History—
19th century. 5. Paleontology—United States—History—19th century.
I. Title. QE707.C63K56 2006 560.92 '273—dc22 2006006469

Printed in the United States of America
10 9 8 7 6 5 4 3 2 1
First Edition

Photo credits are found on page 112.

For Milo, who loves bones
—E.C.K.

CONTENTS

INTRODUCTION

On a bitter cold Wyoming day in 1878, two men hurried over the prairie with shovels and picks. They worked for a famous scientist named O. C. Marsh, and their job was to dig large pits, called quarries, in the prairie of Como Bluff. Beneath the earth lay ancient wonders, lost treasures that Marsh desperately hoped the men would uncover. Leg bones taller than the men themselves. Skulls and teeth from creatures of massive size. Traces of dinosaurs so huge they made elephants look like rabbits.

The two diggers had been careful to keep the boneyard a secret from other scientists and their diggers. They sent messages to Marsh's office in Connecticut only in code. They used false names at all times. If word of this secret got out, the quarries would certainly be mobbed with fossil hunters. The men were not scientists. They were experts only at locating and retrieving bones. What they did know was that dinosaur bones such as these were as valuable as gold, and that a scientist like Marsh would pay well for them. The men did not want to share the bones, or the money Marsh paid, with anyone.

Marsh was also trying to keep Como Bluff a secret for as long as he could, but not because of money. He wanted the boneyard to remain a secret for a different reason. Every time Marsh found a site filled with rare fossils, another man soon came after the specimens himself. The man was another scientist, named Edward Cope. Because they searched the earth to find fossilized skeletons, scientists like Cope and Marsh were called bone hunters. Although Cope and Marsh shared the same profession, they were bitter rivals. In fact, Edward Cope and O. C. Marsh hated each other.

The boneyard of Como Bluff did not stay a secret for long, in spite of everyone's efforts. The diggers reported to Marsh that a stranger had been hanging around their quarries. As Marsh immediately suspected, it was discovered that the stranger worked for Cope. Marsh told his men to do anything they could to thwart Cope's spy. They put up tents over the places where they were digging so that no outsider could see what they had found. After they had excavated and removed a fossil, they locked it in a storehouse, where it could not be seen or stolen by Cope's man. When Marsh's diggers finished removing fossils from a quarry, they took sledgehammers and smashed everything left behind. If Cope or his man came looking, all he would find was dust.

Edward Cope, however, was not so easily stopped.

1

THE BIRTH OF PALEONTOLOGY

Over 65 million years after the last dinosaur died off and the last species became extinct, the world knew almost nothing about dinosaurs. In the nineteenth century, the field of fossil study itself, called paleontology, was a relatively new science. Throughout America's western territories, huge treasure troves of dinosaur bones lay tucked into the earth, waiting to be found. The bones had an unbelievable tale to tell—a story of animals more huge and powerful than anyone imagined possible. It was a story that would be dug from the earth by the first paleontologists.

Two early paleontologists stand out as much for their feud as for their individual brilliance. Each did work that helped lay the foundation for the study of dinosaurs. Each had an understanding of paleontology well ahead of the times. And although they started out as friends, the hatred they came to feel for one another lasted until their deaths. These paleontologists were Edward Drinker Cope and Othniel Charles Marsh. They spent years trying to destroy each other's scientific reputations, but their names are now forever linked. In the pages of history, they are most often remembered, and written about, together.

The very word "dinosaur" did not exist before the nineteenth century. In 1841, a British scientist named Sir Richard Owen studied some recently discovered fossils and realized that they belonged to an entirely new category of animals. He gave the new category a name: Dinosauria, meaning "terrible lizard." Today most children know the word "dinosaur" before they enter kindergarten, but in 1841, few people even imagined that a race of lizard-like giant animals had once ruled the earth. The discovery of the existence of dinosaurs set the imagination of the public afire, and developments were vividly reported in newspapers. Special scientists, newly called paleontologists, began working to unlock the secrets of fossils. Those fossils held the key to the world of dinosaurs.

Fossils are the remains of a plant or animal that have been preserved in rocks. When an animal skeleton becomes buried in soil, certain parts, such as the teeth and bones, can be hardened by minerals in the earth. The bones then are transformed into rocks, which are called fossils.

While paleontology was a fairly new science in the nineteenth century, people's fascination with fossils seems to be as old as the human race itself. Settlements of early people from the Neanderthal period have provided archaeological evidence that even then humans gathered

and collected fossils. There are examples of Cro-Magnon jewelry, dating 35,000 years back in time, made of shell fossils. In early Greek and Roman writings, scholars pondered the nature and origin of fossils. To some, oversized bones seemed like proof of the existence of giants and dragons. Small fossils were thought to be the remains of petrified snake tongues and meteorites. Certain civilizations believed fossils were made by magic. Others believed fossils had valuable healing powers, curing sores and acting as an antidote to poisons. They were given names based on their appearances, such as sea bean, star seal, and tongue stone. Both Hindus and Native Americans believed that fossils were sacred objects.

Over time, fossil collectors began getting closer to the truth. By the seventeenth century, many people agreed that fossils were the remains

Large fossils like these dinosaur bones found in Wyoming in 1898 might be the source of myths about giants and dragons in many cultures around the world.

of once-living creatures. One hundred years after that, scientists decided that the earth was much older than people had thought. Based on the story of Adam and Eve in the Bible, people calculated that the earth itself was about 6,000 years old. In the eighteenth century, scientists developed a new theory that the earth might be as old as 75,000 years. Today we know that fossils show that there was life on earth more than 3 billion years ago!

Another scientific theory led the way to the rapid growth of paleontology. It was Charles Darwin's theory of evolution. This theory was published in 1859 in his book *On the Origin of Species by Means of Natural Selection*. Darwin asserted that some species gradually changed physical characteristics or features over a long period of time. Some of these new features, such as sharper teeth or longer legs, would make an animal more likely to survive and triumph over predators. Darwin thought animals that developed an advantageous new feature could pass it on to

ON

THE ORIGIN OF SPECIES

BY MEANS OF NATURAL SELECTION,

OR THE

PRESERVATION OF FAVOURED RACES IN THE STRUGGLE
FOR LIFE.

By CHARLES DARWIN, M.A.,

FELLOW OF THE ROYAL, GEOLOGICAL, LINNÆAN, ETC., SOCIETIES;
AUTHOR OF 'JOURNAL OF RESEARCHES DURING H. M. S. BEAGLE'S VOYAGE
ROUND THE WORLD.'

The title page of the first edition of Charles Darwin's 1859 publication *On the Origin of Species,* a book that signaled the beginning of a revolution in scientific thought.

their offspring. Animals of that species without the advantage eventually died off. Ultimately, the surviving species members all possessed the new feature. The species had changed through "natural selection."

The idea of evolution made many people angry because it seemed to oppose the story of creation as it was told in the Bible. The creation story indicated life, including humankind, was created in the form we know it today 6,000 years ago. Darwin's theory of evolution showed life evolving over a much longer period of time. Which idea was correct? The new science of paleontology gave scientists a method by which natural selection could be tested. If enough fossils could be found of the same species, they could be arranged in order of age to display features that had changed over the centuries. This would be proof of evolution.

The United States of America was only sixty-five years old when the word "dinosaur" was coined. The debate over evolution set the stage for the next great leap in science. The field of paleontology was a blank page, awaiting someone to fill it in. A small number of thinkers were up to the challenge. For two of them, the detective work of fossil study would become the greatest fight of their lives.

2

THE CHILDHOOD OF A BONE HUNTER

Marsh and Cope had much more in common than either of them might have liked to admit. When their lives are summed up in the history books, we can see several parallels in their childhoods. The similarities make it surprising that these two like-minded men did not become lifelong friends. In fact, they despised each other so much, just hearing the other's name was practically unbearable.

Othniel Charles Marsh, called O.C., was born in 1831 and lived on a farm outside of Lockport, New York. His mother died when he was three years old, and his large family did not have much money. The Marshes made their living from the land, and on the farm there was no end of chores to be done. As a boy, Marsh often looked for an escape from farmwork to have some fun.

When he met the amateur geologist Colonel Ezekiel Jewett, Marsh discovered there was more to the earth than farming. The soil held minerals—the natural substances that make up rocks—and it also held fossils. The area around Lockport was rich with fossils that had been exposed by blasting during the construction of the Erie Canal locks. There were countless fossils to be found of trilobites, extinct sea creatures resembling a crablike insect. The colonel was very good at locating them, and he taught young Marsh what he knew. Whenever Marsh could get away from his farm chores, he went along with the colonel on mineral-and-fossil-collecting trips. He found these trips fascinating. More than ever, Marsh realized that he did not want to spend his life working as a farmer.

Marsh had attended school, but had never been a good student. When he turned twenty-one, he inherited some money from his mother's estate. To his father's surprise, Marsh decided to use the money for a high school education. Though much older than the other students, Marsh enrolled at Phillips Academy. He got a summer job organizing a mineral collection for a local museum and spent two more summers collecting fossils in Nova Scotia. Eventually, Marsh became a very good student. By the time he graduated from high school in 1856, he was sure that he wanted to spend his life working with minerals and fossils.

Though his father had no money to spare for luxuries such as college, Marsh had somewhere else to turn for help. His uncle George Peabody

George Peabody spent about $9 million on charitable causes—including the education of his nephew O. C. Marsh.

had a vast fortune. Peabody was a man who placed the highest importance on education. He was also a man who enjoyed donating money, as long as he found the cause to be worthwhile. So when Marsh asked for assistance to pay for a college education, Peabody was more than willing to help. With Uncle George paying the way, Marsh was able to attend Yale University, then called Yale College.

Since Peabody gave Marsh spending money as well, Marsh rented himself several rooms in a private home. He lived in one of the rooms and used the others for his growing collection of fossils and minerals. Eventually, his collection grew so large and heavy that his landlady had to prop up his floor from below to prevent it from collapsing under the weight.

Marsh did very well at Yale, and when he graduated, Peabody knew his nephew had great potential in the world of academic science. He agreed to pay for Marsh to study for two more years at Yale's Sheffield Scientific School. Though the Civil War broke out during his first year at the graduate school, Marsh's terrible eyesight prevented him from serving as a soldier. He continued his studies and received a master's degree in 1862.

At the time, few countries had as much to offer scientific scholars as did Germany. Since he could not fight in the war, Marsh decided to visit Germany to take additional classes in geology and biology. Again his uncle paid all of Marsh's expenses. While in Germany, Marsh heard that Peabody was donating a large amount of money to Harvard University, a rival of Yale. Many children in the Peabody family had attended Harvard, and it was natural for Peabody to want to make a financial gift to the college.

But Marsh wanted nothing more than to become a professor at Yale. He felt his future lay there. Marsh knew that Yale would be thrilled if they received a donation as large as the one Harvard would be getting. Marsh was somehow able to convince his uncle to give the same amount of money to Yale for their science program. Marsh then wrote to Yale to tell them of their good fortune, and to take the opportunity to confirm his own interest in becoming a Yale professor.

Yale was pleased to accept both the money and the services of Marsh as their first professor of paleontology. The college would get a new museum (to be named after Peabody) and one of paleontology's most promising young scholars on their faculty. By 1866, Marsh had his new job. But Yale did not have many real fossils for students to study and needed a good fossil collection. Marsh knew the Peabody Museum must be provided with a major fossil collection of the best, the oldest, and the most unusual specimens.

Marsh decided to go west and get them.

Yale University's Peabody Museum of Natural History in New Haven, Connecticut, was founded in 1866 through the financial support of George Peabody, but it was Marsh's paleontological contributions that established the museum's world-class collections.

3

A YOUNG NATURALIST

Cope, too, grew interested in the scientific world when he was just a boy. Born outside of Philadelphia in 1840, Edward Drinker Cope lived with his wealthy Quaker family in a beautiful stone house named Fairfield. The founder of the Quaker religion, George Fox, felt that studying plants and natural things was a good way to know God better. The Copes believed this as well, and Cope's father made sure his

Edward Drinker Cope, at the age of ten in 1850.

children's education included nature study and walks in Fairfield's gardens.

Cope visited Boston with his father when he was six and kept a diary of the trip that included drawings and descriptions of the animals he saw. Two years later, he visited the Academy of Natural Sciences in Philadelphia. The sketches that he made of museum specimens showed that young Cope had an unusual gift. At the age of eight, he was already thinking, writing, and drawing like a true scientist.

Though the Copes had plenty of money, Alfred Cope felt it important that his son earn a living. He wanted Edward to be a gentleman farmer, working the land not because he needed money but because such work was respectable.

Like Marsh, however, Cope had different ideas about his future. When he was twenty years old, Cope convinced his father to let him attend some science classes at the University of Pennsylvania. The classes were taught by Joseph Leidy, a well-known naturalist and expert on the paleontology of vertebrates—animals with backbones. Leidy was the field's first expert and is now often considered the "father" of paleontology. Cope was enthralled by Leidy's lectures. Though little is

Joseph Leidy, seen here teaching at Pennsylvania's Wagner Free Institute, was a pioneer of paleontology. Cope was among his students.

known of how close the student and the teacher became, Leidy was sufficiently impressed by Cope to help him become a member of the Academy of Natural Sciences the following year.

That same year, Cope's father gave him his own farm, but for Cope there was no turning back to that world. He wanted to live a life of science, not farming. Cope decided to rent out his farm and let other people work his land and cultivate his crops. The money that Cope received from the tenants would be enough to pay his bills. This gave Cope what he most wanted—the freedom to pursue his science and study wherever and whenever he chose.

In 1861, Cope traveled to Washington, D.C., to visit the country's most famous scientific institution, the Smithsonian. The Civil War had begun, but most Quakers were pacifists, which meant they deeply opposed warfare and fighting. So Cope did not voluntarily enlist in the Civil War, and hoped that he would not be drafted, or ordered to serve. He used his time at the

Smithsonian and at Philadelphia's Academy of Natural Sciences to improve his education in areas such as the study of plants and animals.

The Smithsonian and the Academy of Natural Sciences in Philadelphia were the United States' two best scientific institutions. At the time, America did not place enormous importance on science, and no other institutions in the country could offer Cope a cutting-edge course of advanced study. The real hotbed of scientific education was in Europe. But traveling to Europe was costly, and the small income Cope earned from his farm was not enough to pay for the trip.

Cope's father agreed to pay for his son to go to Europe and pursue his education there. By this time, Alfred Cope had probably accepted that his headstrong son would never be a farmer. He may also have seen the overseas trip as a way to keep his son far from the ravages of the Civil War. In Europe, Cope visited the most important museums, studied their collections, and learned all that he could from those in charge. One of the subjects Cope studied and learned about most zealously was fossils.

Cope also visited with other students who, like him, had come to Europe to further their scientific education. In 1864, Cope met an American who was studying fossils at the University of Berlin in Germany. The American's name was O. C. Marsh. The two enjoyed a long conversation about science and about their own lives. They parted from that first visit on the best of terms. Neither man had any idea that they would become rivals in a short period of years.

Cope returned home to Philadelphia in 1864 and found work teaching at a Quaker college called Haverford. By 1867, Cope had married, had a daughter, and grown tired of spending all his time teaching. He had settled on the course that would be his life's passion, and he was ready to enter the working world of paleontology, collecting and researching rather than teaching.

The stage was set for Cope and Marsh to begin their field-changing work. Their different

By the age of thirty, Cope had grown tired of teaching. He was ready to concentrate on fieldwork.

approaches in establishing themselves mirrored the differences in their personalities. Marsh was a man who understood the value of connections,

and he knew how to play the political games necessary to win support in the scholastic world.
He was formal, refined, and genteel, and had a
keen instinct for choosing the right people to
win over to his side. Cope, on the other hand,
had less patience and less opportunity to win
himself a place in the political network. He felt
his work should speak for itself. He was moody
and obsessive, and though he could be generous
and helpful to younger scholars, he was argu-
mentative with those who felt they were his
equal. His emotions often got the better of him.
He tended to brood when he felt he had been
insulted. While Marsh excelled in creating and
maintaining beneficial and peaceful relation-
ships with his peers, Cope seemed to have great
difficulty in keeping peace with anyone. In this
way, they were very different indeed.

But while their personalities differed, young
Cope and Marsh had a good deal in common.
Both spent their childhoods on farms, exploring
the natural world. Both resisted their fathers'

wishes that they become farmers. Both traveled to Europe to get the best education in science. Both returned home to college teaching positions. And both realized that they did not just want to study fossils—they wanted to search for and obtain new specimens themselves. They could have been the best of friends.

Instead, they became lifelong enemies.

4
A FEUD IS BORN

The beginning of Cope and Marsh's feud stems from events rooted in 1868, the year Cope and his family moved to Haddonfield, New Jersey.

Haddonfield was located near large deposits of marl, a claylike substance formed from ancient ocean sediments. Since marl was useful as a fertilizer, in many local areas it was dug up and collected so that it could be sold. Digging of this kind often exposed fossils, and this is why Cope wanted to live nearby. He intended to hunt for fossils, study them, and publish his findings. He also knew that in 1787, America's first dinosaur fossil had been found in New Jersey. That fossil was only a small fragment of a skeleton and was not identified as a dinosaur until many years later.

In 1858, Joseph Leidy removed a much larger portion of a skeleton from a marl pit in Haddonfield. The fossil skeleton was *Hadrosaurus*, an enormous, plant-eating dinosaur thought to reach almost forty feet in length. The skeleton was later reconstructed by Benjamin Waterhouse Hawkins and became the first dinosaur skeleton to be displayed in a museum. Today reconstructed dinosaur skeletons are found in most major natural-history museums, but in the nineteenth century, the sight of the reassembled *Hadrosaurus* towering over the visitors must have been awe-inspiring. It gave people their first real look into the dinosaur world.

This *Hadrosaurus* was the first dinosaur skeleton to ever be displayed in a museum. The man standing beneath the towering dinosaur might be Benjamin Waterhouse Hawkins, who reassembled Leidy's fossil discoveries.

In 1866, Cope made his own first dinosaur find. Like Leidy's *Hadrosaurus*, Cope's discovery came from the Haddonfield marl pits. Cope regularly kept in touch with the men who worked for companies that dug marl from the earth, such as the West Jersey Marl Company. Cope made sure that any worker who found an interesting fossil would let him know at once. Since Cope was always willing to pay for fossils that looked unusual, the workers were happy to help him.

When Cope visited the West Jersey marl pits in 1866, he was astonished by what awaited him. A worker had found a giant claw and a leg bone. Cope was amazed at the sight—they were bigger than any fossilized bones he had ever seen. Making a guess from the size of the leg, Cope calculated that the animal it belonged to would have measured over twenty feet in length. Cope determined that the fossilized bones belonged to a large, meat-eating dinosaur with powerful claws. He named the dinosaur *Laelaps aquilunguis,* meaning "eagle-clawed terrible leaper." It was the most important find since Leidy's *Hadrosaurus.*

Since their meeting in Berlin five years earlier, Cope and Marsh had exchanged letters with one another. Now Marsh came to visit Cope at his Haddonfield home. During the visit, Cope brought Marsh to several of the marl-pit-digging companies whose workers aided Cope by putting aside unusual fossil specimens. Marsh was fascinated to see the pits where *Hadrosaurus* and *Laelaps* had been found. What Cope did not know was that Marsh had privately met with the owner of the marl pit where *Laelaps* was discovered. During that meeting, Marsh made a secret arrangement with the owner, perhaps offering more money than Cope. The result was that all newly found fossils of interest would be sent to Marsh at Yale instead of to Cope. Cope was not immediately aware that his source of fossils had been poached.

That same year, Cope obtained another

intriguing fossil from an entirely different source. The specimen was not a dinosaur but a plesiosaur—an ancient reptile that lived in the sea during the Late Cretaceous Period. The fossil had been discovered in Kansas and sent to Philadelphia's Academy of Natural Sciences, where Cope was able to study and reconstruct it. The crates delivered to the academy contained over one hundred little bones that Cope had to clean and identify. Once this task was completed, he had to piece the bones together to make a skeleton. It took many months of painstaking work, but almost a year after he had opened the crates, Cope finally completed the reconstruction. The skeleton was thirty-five feet in length, with a long, flexible neck and tail. Cope named the plesiosaur *Elasmosaurus*.

As soon as Cope's reconstruction was finished, he wrote and illustrated a paper about the skeleton. The paper and illustrations were published in a science journal for other scientists to

Cope eventually became the mentor of Charles R. Knight, a painter who devoted his career to imagining extinct animals. Here is Knight's 1897 depiction of *Elasmosaurus*—with its head on the *correct* end.

read. Many people were very excited about the skeleton, and Cope was enormously proud of his work.

Marsh was eager to see this reconstruction,

and he came to Philadelphia to visit Cope at the academy shortly after the work on *Elasmosaurus* was completed. Marsh examined every inch of Cope's reconstruction. Afterward, he made a startling claim. Cope, he said, had made a major error in the reconstruction. *Elasmosaurus* had both a very long neck and a very long tail. Marsh determined that Cope had put the skull on the wrong end of the skeleton. Instead of putting it on the neck, Cope had placed it on the tail!

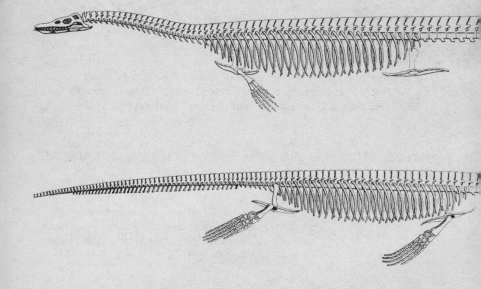

Expert Joseph Leidy was called in to consult, and his conclusion was the same as Marsh's. Cope had indeed put the head on the tail of the plesiosaur. It was a hugely embarrassing mistake for Cope. He tried to get back every copy of the journal that had published his papers and drawings, illustrations he now knew to contain a spectacular error. But not only would Marsh not give back his own copy, he also told other scientists about Cope's mistake. Cope felt that

Top: *Elasmosaurus* as first envisioned by Cope.
Bottom: A correct version of *Elasmosaurus*, after Marsh pointed out that Cope had placed the creature's skull at the end of its tail.

Marsh had gone out of his way to ensure that he looked stupid. For Cope, it was a very public humiliation.

Later that same year, Cope finally realized he was not receiving as many fossils from the West Jersey marl pits as he had previously. Before long, he discovered that most of the fossils were being sent to Marsh. For Cope, this amounted to little more than outright stealing. He felt that he had shared his marl pits with Marsh in the spirit of professional friendship. Marsh had repaid him by poaching the fossil supply for himself.

In this short but crucial period of time, Cope and Marsh had gone from polite friends sharing similar scientific interests to competitors. They were still on cordial terms, occasionally speaking and exchanging letters. But the relationship was now excruciatingly formal and always underlined with mutual distrust. Cope suspected Marsh of gross dishonesty. Marsh suspected Cope of massive incompetence. The most important work in dinosaur paleontology in the world was about to take place in the United States. A large part of it would be carried out by Edward Cope and O. C. Marsh. Together they would have been the ultimate dream team of intellect and ambition.

5

INTO THE WEST

In 1868, Marsh decided to go west and search for an entirely new source of fossils to fill Yale's classrooms and the Peabody Museum. The idea of personally organizing and participating in such an expedition was ahead of its time. Scientists of Marsh's day did not usually go out and hunt for objects to study. They hired people to bring specimens to them and did much of their work indoors. But Marsh did not want to rely on the specimens a handful of amateur geologists and marl-pit workers might send his way. No one had the level of expertise that he did, and he worried that spectacular specimens might be overlooked by others. Marsh determined to do the bone hunting himself.

The American scientific community was small, and news traveled fast. Marsh would certainly have heard the claims of fur traders who had gone up the Missouri River and seen clusters of enormous bones sticking out of the earth. Some of the traders had even dug out a few smaller bones, which were eventually purchased by Joseph Leidy. These bones were the first hint that there might be rich fossil beds located in the American West, and that, equally important, they might contain dinosaur bones.

At this time, most fossil study had centered on the bones of ancient mammal species. It had been only about twenty-five years since Richard Owen had isolated a new reptilian species and named it "dinosaur." Since that time, very few dinosaur fossils had been found. The two most notable finds, *Hadrosaurus* and *Laelaps* (later renamed *Dryptosaurus*), had been discovered by Leidy and Cope, respectively.

Now it seemed possible that the American West might be the place where more dinosaur fossils could finally be found. Railroad workers building train tracks across Nebraska and Wyoming also reported seeing huge numbers of old bones scattered about. Marsh knew something significant was out there, and he intended to be the one to find it.

That year, the American Association for the Advancement of Science offered a program for scientists that included a train trip on the Union Pacific line. The line was being built westward at the same time that the Central Pacific line was extending its tracks east. The goal, ultimately reached in 1869 in Utah, was to have the two train lines meet, thereby providing transcontinental rail travel. In the summer of 1868, the Union Pacific line had been completed through

The Central Pacific Railroad opened up the West to pioneers—and pioneering scientists like Cope and Marsh.

western Wyoming, in the area of Green River. The transcontinental railroad would give paleontologists and geologists safe and reliable transportation into areas of the West that just decades ago were reachable only by horse or covered wagon.

Marsh was anxious to make the train trip, and to visit Nebraska and Wyoming himself. During a brief stop at the station in Antelope, Wyoming, Marsh saw with his own eyes the bleached bones lying all over the ground. He was unable to investigate closely because the train had to leave, but he paid the local station-master to collect any samples that looked interesting and hold them for him.

Marsh picked up the bones on the return trip through Antelope. When he examined what the stationmaster had collected, his suspicions were confirmed. Though they were not dinosaur bones, they were rare and valuable fossils of a number of extinct animals, including a tiny ancestor of today's horse. Marsh decided he must plan a major expedition to the West for the summer of 1870.

Marsh's preparation for the trip was briefly interrupted when a box of fossils intended for Yale somehow ended up being sent to Edward Cope instead. It seemed unlikely to Marsh that this was an innocent error. Exactly how or why it happened is unknown, but Cope sent a letter to Marsh immediately, explaining that it was all a misunderstanding. Marsh was extremely annoyed that his fossils had gone astray and ended up on Cope's desk. Though Cope indicated he had forwarded the fossils on to Marsh, he almost certainly examined them first. But since Marsh was to leave for the West in just a few weeks, and since the fossils had been sent to Yale, there was little he could do. In any event, if Marsh's trip went as planned, he would have access to more fossils than Cope could even dream of.

Marsh had a large pool of workers to choose from in the student body of Yale. He easily found eleven strong young men willing to volunteer their digging services in this great western adventure. Marsh also contacted the U.S. Army to request a military escort for his group. His concern for their personal safety was well founded— it was a time of terrible unrest for many Indian tribes. The government was trying to take away Indian land, causing great anger among them. The Sioux and Cheyenne in particular were considered actively hostile that summer.

Marsh's group took the train to North Platte, Nebraska. From there they went to Fort McPherson, where they were planning to pick up their military escort. The army had hired the famous frontiersman and scout Buffalo Bill

Cody to guide and protect Marsh and his men. But before he could start work, Cody and a party of antelope hunters were attacked by twelve Sioux warriors. Cody managed to escape the flying arrows, but another hunter was not so lucky. When they returned to Fort McPherson, one Sioux warrior was dead and

The frontiersman known as Buffalo Bill was supposed to accompany Marsh's first western expedition, but he was reassigned to deal with rebellious Sioux before the expedition was under way.

one antelope hunter had an arrow still sticking out of him. The army decided it was more important for Cody to try to capture the Sioux warriors than to help hunt for old bones.

Buffalo Bill Cody's brush with death did not cause Marsh to change his plans. With a new scout and several Pawnee guides, Marsh and his group of students left the safety of the fort and traveled on horseback over the hilly prairies of Nebraska. Everyone needed to remain constantly on full alert because the tall grass could easily hide Sioux warriors, or rattlesnakes, or pools of quicksand near the river.

They traveled pioneer-style, carting all their supplies by wagon and making camp each night. They pitched tents close to their campfire and slept as the temperature dropped. After feeling cold all night, they resumed travel each day in blistering temperatures that reached as high as 110 degrees. Only Marsh did not seem bothered by the conditions. He talked so much about rocks and fossils his men began to think the lessons were more torturous than the weather. The one time Marsh's lessons stopped was when they reached a site he thought promising. Then the real work began. They dug and chipped their way through clay and rock, discovering fossils of ancient rhinos, mastodons, and horses.

As Marsh and his students dug, they saw smoke signals in the distance. The Sioux were sending messages to each other. Later, when the sky filled with black smoke, Marsh realized that the Sioux had set fire to the prairie. The fire raged toward his camp. The approaching danger finally forced Marsh away from his digging. He and his men left their work and ran along the ground, beating out flames with blankets. But the fire was too powerful, and it was clear they could not put it out themselves. Just in time, the clouds opened. The rain put out the fire, and Marsh ordered his men back to work.

In spite of the unplanned complications and danger, Marsh had come to the right place to dig. There seemed to be fossils everywhere. But

when he tried to show his Pawnee scouts the
hardened bones, the Indians would not touch
them. Their legends said that the bones were
the remains of a race of ancient giants. Marsh
stopped his digging to give the Pawnee a quick

Marsh (standing, center) led the first Yale College Scientific Expedition
into dangerous territory in 1870. The teacher and his students were
accompanied by a military escort and were away from home for nearly
six full months.

paleontology lesson. He showed them an ancient horse bone he had found in the ground, then pointed to one of the Pawnee horses to show where the same bone was located on the live animal. The ancient bone had come from the same kind of animal as these horses. From then on, the Pawnee joined in the bone hunt and brought Marsh many fossils. They began to call him the "Bone Medicine Man." Marsh lived and breathed for his precious fossils. That summer was probably one of the happiest times of his life.

On the trip, Marsh gathered six crates of specimens to ship back to Yale on the railway. As the first scientific fossil expedition organized in the United States, the trip also brought Marsh some publicity. But locating the fossils and digging them out of the ground had just been the first step. Now Marsh had to clean and study them—hundreds of puzzle pieces that he must fit together. Only when he had completed each puzzle could he write papers about what he had found. When his work was published in scientific journals, he would become the most famous paleontologist in the country. And there would not be a thing Cope could do about it.

It is not at all surprising, then, that Edward Cope decided it was time to organize his own expedition into the West.

6

IN MARSH'S FOOTSTEPS

Edward Cope had never seen anything like the grass plains of Kansas. Looking out the train window, he watched buffalo herds fill the prairie as far as the eye could see. He also saw enormous flowers with stalks as tall as a man. But Edward Cope was not traveling out west to take in the pretty sights. O. C. Marsh had already managed to organize his second bone-hunting trip out west. At this very moment, Marsh and his party of Yale diggers were excavating on the plains. If Cope was ever going to catch up with Marsh's collection, which already contained hundreds and hundreds of rare and unusual fossils, he was going to have to work fast.

Following Marsh, Cope started with a visit to Fort Wallace. He knew that Marsh and his party had been there just months before. At the fort, Cope was able to hire a few soldiers to escort his group. He also, to his great delight, met one of Marsh's former guides and promptly hired him as well. Now Cope not only had protection and a guide, he would also be able to learn exactly what areas Marsh had already picked over and what he had found. And if it made Marsh angry to learn Cope had poached his former guide, all the better. Cope felt very glad about his good luck.

Cope arrived at the Kansas fossil beds that Marsh's Yale group had excavated. It was the fall of 1871, and Cope was at last in a position to dig some quarries of his own. Why did he choose to begin his expedition on ground that Marsh had recently left? The memory of the Haddonfield marl pits might still have gnawed at Cope. Perhaps Cope wished to show that he, too, could steal onto someone else's territory. In reality, the area was so rich with fossils that no matter how many were dug up, countless others still remained in the ground.

The area of western Kansas where Cope was searching had been a sea during the Cretaceous Period. Left behind was evidence of the flying pterodactyls, ocean reptiles such as mosasaurs, and coastal dinosaurs that had once lived there. The fossils were plentiful, and Cope was thrilled with his finds—particularly a pterodactyl with a twenty-foot wingspan. Pterodactyls were reptiles that had evolved into winged creatures of great power. In Europe, the only pterodactyls found had been small, about the size of a robin. Cope was not the first to unearth a giant pterodactyl fossil—in fact, Marsh himself had already found a bone belonging to a very large pterodactyl. But the fossil Cope found was even bigger. It was a magnificent discovery that scored Cope an important point. His specimen was *bigger* than Marsh's.

Cope worked long hours digging and collecting his fossils, but he always took time to write fanciful letters about his adventures to his five-year-old daughter, Julia. There were many amazing sights and sounds he wanted to describe to her. Strange, fat, squirrel-like creatures called prairie dogs peeked out of their holes to watch the diggers. Cope promised to try to catch one for Julia. He described the sound of coyotes howling in the dark of night. He told her he had raced buffalo on horseback and had been chased by wolves. He also described the numerous rattlesnakes he saw, snakes whose bite could kill a man. With great satisfaction, he told Julia he had even killed a rattlesnake himself and put its remains in a bag. He promised to bring it home so little Julia could see it with her own eyes.

What he did not mention to her in his letters was that his greatest enemy, O. C. Marsh, was some 500 miles away digging for fossils in Wyoming.

Cope met a land agent named Webb, who in his work had come to know a great deal about the Kansas landscape, including areas laden with fossils. Cope's group went along with Webb to Hays, Kansas. Hays was a notorious Wild West town that had been home to Wild Bill Hickok, widely known as the most deadly gunslinger alive, a man that might shoot his own grandmother if she looked at him wrong. But Cope was not interested in Wild West stories, or Hays's cowboys and outlaws. With Webb's help, Cope planned to hunt for fossils around the nearby Saline River. As they rode to the area, they were intercepted by a band of Cheyenne Indians and their chief, White Wolf. The Indians wanted food. Wishing to make friends, Cope's group took them along to Hays, making sure they were well fed and provided for.

Cope's group eventually reached the Saline

River safely, making a camp from which Cope
searched for fossils, hunted for food, and wrote
papers about his scientific findings. Cope did not
want to stay away from his home and family
much longer, and in December he decided to pack
up and leave. However, he was already planning
how and when he could return to the West.

Edward Cope was a member of the U.S.
Geological and Geographical Survey of the Territories. Because of this, the government sent
him as the official paleontologist to Wyoming
Territory six months later, in June of 1872. At
this time, there were still large areas of land in
the United States that were unmapped. Many
Americans were homesteading—building new
homes on the frontier and driving Indians off the
land. Homesteaders were required to file official
claims with the government describing the par-
cel of land they were taking, and precise maps
were necessary to show the features of these
claims. The U.S. Geological Survey organized
trips to make these detailed measurements and

maps. It also sent paleontologists to learn if any of the newly mapped areas had mineral deposits or gold beneath the soil. For Cope, this particular assignment from the Geological Survey gave him a welcome opportunity to search for fossils in the rich earth around Fort Bridger in Wyoming, where Marsh had made significant finds the year before. As part of an official government undertaking, Cope was permitted to obtain supplies and food from the army.

When Cope first searched the Fort Bridger area, he quickly learned that its reputation as a fossil treasure trove was entirely accurate. As in Kansas the previous year, Cope was able to hire one of Marsh's former diggers, Sam Smith. Sadly for Cope, Smith turned out to be a better spy than fossil hunter. Smith secretly wrote to Marsh to keep him updated on where Cope was digging and exactly what kind of fossils he was finding.

For the men working, the days were unbearably hot and the nights freezing cold. Fresh

Cope's sketch of the horned lizard *Agathaumas,* from the sketchbook of his 1872 expedition, was based on very few fossils. Today many scientists believe Cope, in 1872, had actually discovered *Triceratops* fossils. *Triceratops* was officially named by Marsh, but not until 1889.

drinking water was not easy to come by. Several of Cope's pack mules wandered off and got lost, and one of his men stole some supplies and ran away. In spite of these difficulties, Cope was able to find many remarkable specimens. His spirits were probably improved by the arrival of his wife and daughter, for whom he had rented a small house near Fort Bridger. Now his family could spend the summer together while he worked.

Cope was collecting such a huge number of

specimens that he did not want to ship them home and delay publishing his analysis of them. He began working on his papers at night, after many hours of digging. The frantic pace took its toll on Cope's health, but he had good reason to feel so pressed to rush his work. He was no longer the only paleontologist hunting fossils in Wyoming.

Several weeks after Cope traveled to Wyoming, Joseph Leidy arrived. Two surgeons posted at Fort Bridger were friendly with Leidy and had often sent him fossils they discovered in the area. They had invited Leidy to visit them so that he could personally examine the local fossils. Leidy was more than happy to accept the invitation.

Though Cope and Leidy were not rivals, they were also not as close as they had once been. Leidy did not like Cope's confrontational way of dealing with other scientists and scholars. Cope always seemed to be arguing with people. Someone who knew them both described Leidy as a man who kept the peace with his peers no matter what it cost, and Cope as a man who kept arguing no matter what the price. Though Leidy had no interest in being first or beating anyone to a discovery, Cope could not have been happy to have him on the scene. To him, Leidy was simply more competition about which to worry.

In New Haven, Marsh had been keeping up to date on the progress of the digs in Wyoming by way of secret reports from employees and associates like Sam Smith. Though he might have preferred to stay home and work in solitude, the reports he was getting made it clear he needed to get to Bridger Basin as soon as possible. The final straw for Marsh was learning that Sam Smith had suddenly changed his mind and decided to stop spying on Cope, and instead start working *for* him in earnest. Marsh knew he had to get out to Wyoming Territory. The following month, Marsh arrived in Kansas, then set out with four of his Yale students for Wyoming.

There were now three parties of paleontologists hunting fossils within several miles of
each other. All three were about to discover a
very important type of dinosaur fossil, causing
the simmering war to rapidly boil over.

7

WAR OF NAMES

By 1872, Cope and Marsh had already had several conflicts. Now the unpleasantness was about to escalate. They did not fight each other physically, face to face. They fought each other on paper, using words to wound one another. They fought to convince other scientists that only one of them deserved respect. They used the most popular scientific journals of the day as their battlefield, with accusations as their weapons.

When a scientist makes a discovery or completes an important experiment, he or she publishes a paper on the work in a scientific journal. Almost every other scientist doing similar work reads that journal, which is printed and sold like a magazine. Publishing papers is not just a way for scientists to show off their best work—it is the accepted way to get credit for research or discoveries. Anyone can claim to have found a bone from a new species of animal, but whoever publishes a paper on that bone first is the one who gets official credit for the discovery. One of the privileges given to a scientist who has officially discovered a new animal is the right to give it a name. As long as scientists keep to a few rules, they can name an animal anything they want.

In the nineteenth century, the accepted procedure to classify and name an animal used by the scientific community was called the Linnaeus system. It required that a name have two parts:

the "genus," or general animal family, and the "species," or the very specific type of animal within that family. Using those rules, a scientist could devise genus and species names based on a physical characteristic of the animal, the location in which it was discovered, or even the name of a person.

In friendlier times, Cope and Marsh had actually named fossils for each other. But the days of *Ptyonius marshii* and *Mosasaurus copeanus* were long gone. As far as Cope and Marsh were concerned, there was now a race to discover and name an animal first. The ultimate contest, of course, would be who could name the most. This competition eventually caused an extraordinary amount of confusion.

In the summer of 1872, Cope, Marsh, and Leidy were all excavating in Wyoming Territory within several miles of each other. They did not communicate or share news of what they were finding. Cope and Marsh did everything they could to keep the details of their digs secret. So when all three paleontologists discovered fossilized remains from species of a large plant-eating animal, they did not tell one another.

The new discovery was a rhinoceros-sized creature with several horns on its skull. Joseph Leidy examined the fossil skeleton he had found and gave the creature the genus name *Uintatherium*, or "beast of the Uinta Mountains." Two weeks later, knowing nothing of Leidy's work, Cope discovered a similar specimen and named it *Loxolophodon*, or "crested tooth." About the same time, possibly even the same day, Marsh also came across a fossil of a specimen. He named his *Dinoceras*, or "terrible horn."

To further confuse matters, Cope next discovered another species of the animal and named it *Eobasileus*, or "dawn ruler." Each paleontologist believed he had discovered the rhino-like creature first, and that he had the sole right to give it a name. Each published papers

The rivalry between Cope and Marsh exploded over who should provide the name for an extinct horned mammal that had been discovered simultaneously by Leidy and the two younger scientists.

on what he had found. It was only when the papers appeared that they realized they had all discovered fossils at roughly the same time.

Cope and Marsh were furious to learn they had written about the same creature. Both published new articles claiming they had been first. Each accused the other of being wrong or, worse, of making up information.

Joseph Leidy did not want to be in the middle of this fight. Getting credit was not of great importance to him. He just wanted to find and study new bones. So Leidy did not publish any more papers himself, and he did not accuse Cope or Marsh of having flawed research. He chose to stay quiet, while Cope and Marsh attacked each other in the journals.

In the next year, Cope and Marsh each published over a dozen articles on the rhino creature. Marsh wrote an article saying Cope had made up fake dates for his papers to create the illusion that he had found the fossil first. Cope was a cheater, Marsh wrote. Cope responded by writing an article saying that Marsh was a liar. They leveled these accusations at each other in journals such as the *American Journal of Science* and the *American Naturalist*. Leidy continued to remain silent about his own claims. Because he was a scientist of the old school, he was not willing to get involved in this messy public battle.

Cope's and Marsh's articles made the country's two most distinguished paleontologists look like a couple of little boys arguing over a game. They kicked the issue back and forth, until the *American Naturalist* finally published its own article, stating it would no longer print any of Cope's or Marsh's arguments on the subject.

Though each had plenty more to say, the subject was, for the time, closed. Both paleontologists made plans to return to the West for more fossil hunting. Ultimately, neither Cope nor Marsh clearly won the first battle over names. The dinosaur is today identified by the genus name *Uintatherium*, the name created by Joseph Leidy. One species of uintathere is now known

as *Eobasileus*, and the larger, general group of animals is often referred to as *Dinoceras*. It is now known that Cope's, Marsh's, and Leidy's finds were three separate species of the same uintathere family.

Cope and Marsh immediately jumped back into the fray. As far as they were concerned, the battle of the dinosaur names had only just begun.

Edward Cope here stands with the skull of the animal that he claimed the right to name *Loxolophodon*.

8
THE DISCOVERY OF GIANTS

In the years following the name wars of 1872, Cope and Marsh returned to the West as often as time and money allowed. They also continued to hurl accusations of cheating and flawed research at each other. For all their individual success, both paleontologists were aware that the most important piece of the fossil puzzle had yet to be found—the location of a major source of dinosaur bones. Though each had made significant dinosaur discoveries, a large portion of

Cope's and Marsh's finds was of mammal fossils. No one had yet located more than an individual dinosaur bone or two at a time, and even these specimens were considered rare. Sooner or later, someone would find an area where great numbers of dinosaur fossils lay buried. The paleontologist who discovered that location would certainly become famous all over the world.

In the summer of 1876, Cope was digging in Montana, hoping to find a dinosaur boneyard. With his fellow fossil collectors Charles Sternberg and J. C. Isaac, Cope had come to the Judith River, which had been named during the Lewis and Clark expedition some seventy years earlier for William Clark's sweetheart. Near the river, Cope found the skull of a horned dinosaur. He had collected an enormous number of mammal fossils on the trip, but this was clearly his greatest find. He named the animal *Monoclonius crassus*. But it was an isolated find—he unearthed no other specimens like it in the area.

By the end of September, Cope and his group

managed to drag the 1,200 pounds of fossils they had collected to Cow Island, where the only downriver ferry stopped. Cope suspected that somewhere in the western soil lay a great dinosaur treasure trove, just waiting to be found. After he returned home, his suspicions were confirmed by the news of an astonishing discovery made by a minister in Colorado.

Arthur Lakes was an amateur geologist who enjoyed walking through the Denver countryside collecting minerals and fossils. In March 1877, he saw something in the ground so remarkable he could not believe his eyes. At first he thought it was a section of petrified tree, but he soon realized that he had found a vertebra, a bony section of the spine, that measured

In 1877, Arthur Lakes stumbled upon the "bones of monsters" in Colorado, and he soon began sending his findings to Marsh.

almost three feet around! The creature with a vertebra that size would have to be a giant.

As a serious amateur collector, Lakes knew the names of the two most important paleontologists in the country. He wrote to O. C. Marsh to tell him what he had found. Strangely, he received no reply at first. Marsh may not have taken the letter seriously. Lakes continued to collect bones in the area, and eventually he wrote to Cope. Lakes knew he was on to something incredibly important, and he needed a serious paleontologist to determine what exactly he had found. Marsh or Cope, Lakes did not really care which. As it happened, both Cope and Marsh wrote back to Lakes at around the same time to confirm their interest in buying the vertebra fossil. Unfortunately for Cope, Lakes decided to sell it to Marsh.

Naturally, both paleontologists wanted to get their own diggers to Colorado as soon as possible. In this case, it made more sense for them to hire others to collect the fossils rather than traveling to Colorado in person. The specimens would be shipped back east for examination. This allowed the two paleontologists to spend all of their time in their workshops studying the fossils and writing about them. Since priority for all discoveries went to whoever published his findings first, finishing papers quickly was now Cope and Marsh's main concern.

In a rare instance of agreement, Cope and Marsh wanted the news of what Lakes had found to remain top-secret. Neither wanted any additional competition on the Colorado dinosaur hunt. Princeton University, for example, was becoming a major collector of fossils and might desire to send its own digger to the site. The less the scientific community was told, the better. But as it happened, it was already too late for secrecy.

The newspapers had seized upon a story of "bones of monsters" being found. The news caused a rush of diggers to hurry to Colorado. The frenzy has been compared to that generated by the 1849 gold rush. There weren't many qualified paleontologists in America, but there were plenty of brawny men who could dig up fossils and sell them to the highest bidder.

Lakes continued to personally collect bones for Marsh. But Cope now had his own man, O. W. Lucas, collecting fossils in Colorado and shipping them back east. For Cope and Marsh, almost every shipment they received contained the bones of a new species of dinosaur, each one seemingly larger than the last. As usual, they argued through their published papers that what the other had discovered was flawed or inaccurate in some way. But the frenzy of activity left little time for bickering.

There were plenty of dinosaur bones to go around. Marsh's first major victory was a dinosaur he named *Titanosaurus*—a big-boned plant-eater measuring over forty feet long. Marsh was thrilled that *Titanosaurus* beat out Cope's record for the largest skeleton ever found. But Marsh didn't keep the new record for long. Cope soon announced his discovery of *Camarasaurus*. It was larger than Marsh's giant by at least ten feet. Cope followed this up with an even bigger skeleton of a plant-eater with a snakelike neck. Then Marsh found a dinosaur that, though smaller, captured everyone's interest.

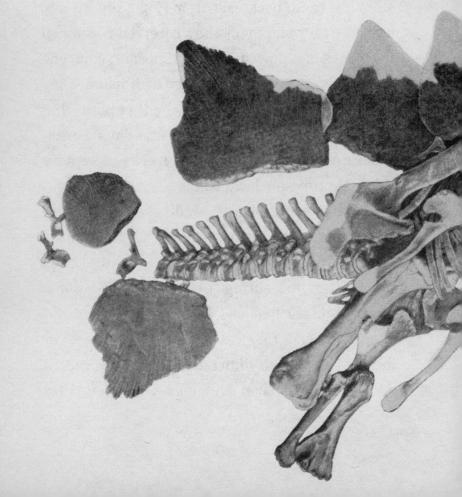

When Marsh first unpacked the crate, he immediately noticed a row of spiky spines. Little by little, he pieced together the other bones that formed this armored creature, including a row of wedge-shaped plates. When he finished, he looked upon an animal the likes of which no

Marsh took a jumble of Colorado fossils and fit them together to create the first reconstruction of *Stegosaurus*.

one had ever seen. He estimated this dinosaur would have measured at least twenty feet long and weighed two tons. With the flat plates on its back, it certainly had the most striking appearance of any dinosaur yet found. Marsh named his new dinosaur *Stegosaurus*.

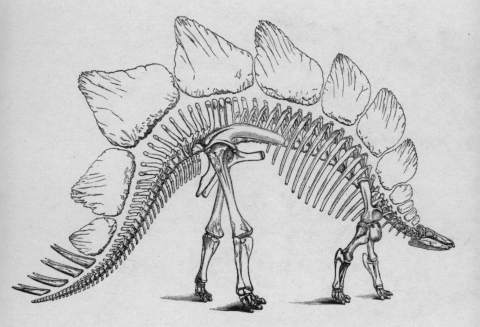

With its arched back lined with bony plates, *Stegosaurus* was an unusual specimen even by the standards of paleontology.

Like a nasty virus, the competitive rivalry between Cope and Marsh soon spread to the men who worked for them. Cope and Marsh encouraged their workers to spy on other camps and report back their findings by telegraph, using coded names. Irritated by the success of Cope's diggers in finding large dinosaurs, Marsh tried to lure Cope's chief collector, Lucas, away. Fortunately for Cope, Lucas remained loyal to his employer. Marsh would have to find another way to get on the inside track. An opportunity soon presented itself.

When two men using false names contacted Marsh with the claim that they had found a second trove of massive bones in Wyoming, Marsh sent the men money to purchase the bones and to buy their silence. He would do anything he had to in order to keep this new boneyard for himself.

As if all this activity wasn't enough, in 1877 Cope and Marsh found something new to fight about.

9

A DEVASTATING BLOW

While Marsh's two men were secretly digging in the new boneyard in Como Bluff, Wyoming, things were happening back in Washington, D.C., that would affect the entire field of paleontology.

The U.S. Geological and Geographical Survey of the Territories was a jackpot for paleontologists like Cope because it offered government-funded opportunities to dig and collect specimens. The government paid for all of the traveling and supplies, and sometimes even gave a small salary to the paleontologist, whose official job was to write reports on the rocks and minerals being found. While doing this work, the paleontologist of course often came across fossils. As long as they completed their official work, survey pale-ontologists could keep all the fossils they found. Cope had been hired many times to work on government surveys. He had come to depend on these jobs.

Though Cope had started life in relative wealth, and Marsh had started without much money of his own, their situations had reversed. After quitting his teaching job, Cope had spent a good deal of his own money financing his work, and his family money had dwindled away. Marsh had inherited money from his uncle George Peabody, drew a salary from Yale University, and had successfully worked himself into the old-boy network, which brought him prestige, elected positions in academic societies, and fund-ing for his projects. As the years went by, Marsh spent less and less of his own money on research, while Cope spent more and more. For Cope, participating in government-funded surveys provided one of the few ways he could afford to continue hunting fossils.

Cope found so many fossils to study on surveys that he wrote the first volume of a major book on paleontology that many called "Cope's bible." Cope considered this book, and the volumes that he intended would follow, to be his life's work. Because it resulted from duties he performed on official surveys, the government paid to have the first volume of Cope's book printed and bound. Cope could never have afforded to do so himself.

In 1878, Congress decided to rethink how they organized land surveys, and they turned to Marsh, who was then the acting president of the National Academy of Sciences, for an expert opinion. He told Congress that they were spending too much money on their land surveys and

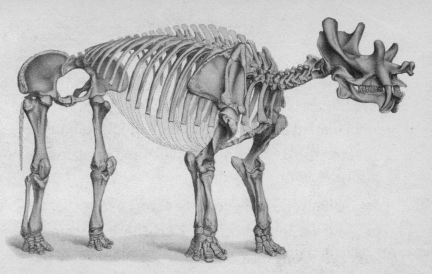

In 1886, the U.S. Geological Survey published Marsh's book on the group of extinct mammals that he called Dinocerata. At the time, Cope found it financially impossible to publish his own work.

hiring too many different people. He recommended that there be only one official government survey party with one chief paleontologist, and suggested himself for the job. By doing this, Marsh not only got himself an influential salaried government job, he also effectively stripped Cope of much of his ability to hunt fossils. In his new position, Marsh could make sure that Cope never received work on a government-funded land survey again.

This was by far the worst damage Marsh had done to Cope. Without the prospect of government-funded work, Cope might never be able to afford to travel out west and hunt fossils again.

Soon Cope received even worse news. Since he now no longer worked on the government surveys, Congress decided they would not pay to publish the second volume of his "bible." Everything Cope had discovered, everything he'd learned, was already painstakingly written and illustrated. But Cope could not afford to publish volume two himself. Without the government's help, the rest of his greatest and most influential work would never be printed. Edward Cope felt his life was being destroyed. But he was not ready to give up the fight. In fact, he had just learned something quite interesting: the location of Marsh's secret dig in Como Bluff.

Marsh's two sources in Wyoming were correct in their claim that they had found something incalculably important. There was indeed a major hot spot of gigantic dinosaur bones in Como Bluff. When Marsh examined the first bones his sources sent, he knew this was the find he had dreamed of. He sent one of his best men, S. W. Williston, to the scene, and Williston reported back with astonishing news. The site was enormous—over six miles long and strewn with big bones. But Williston had some bad news as well. At least seven other people had already seen the bones. It would be impossible to keep Como Bluff a secret, since it was already obvious that it was the most fantastic boneyard ever found.

When word of the Como Bluff secret reached Cope, he quickly got his own man to investigate. The man called himself Haines, and told Marsh's diggers he was a grocery seller. But never had a grocery seller seemed so interested in fossils. Marsh's men sent him word of the suspicious stranger, and he replied that they needed to figure out who Haines really was and relay the information to New Haven via a coded telegraph. Haines left the dig site before his identity could be determined, but an air of suspicion and hostility remained. Everyone now seemed to be a potential spy.

By early 1879, Cope had employed one of Marsh's original Como Bluff diggers, who secretly wrote to Cope with updates on everything the Marsh team was finding. In turn, Marsh's men tried to find out where Cope's diggers were working. While searching for the Cope quarries, Marsh's diggers also strove to keep strangers away from their site. Marsh's people were determined that no outsider get even a peek at their work. In at least one instance after excavating a quarry, Marsh's men used sledgehammers to smash to bits all that was left behind. It was said that the order for the destruction came from Marsh himself so there would be no opportunity for a Cope digger to find anything useful there. Marsh's passion for fossils was equaled by his possessiveness. If one of his quarries still contained fossils, Marsh would rather have them shattered than in the hands of anyone else. This is perhaps one of the saddest elements of Cope and Marsh's war— hundreds of fossils destroyed so that no other paleontologist could benefit from studying them.

The feud created yet another problem. Because Cope and Marsh were in such a rush to publish articles, they both began making mistakes. Marsh was sent an amazing skeleton of a plant-eating dinosaur almost seventy feet long. The only problem was that the skeleton was missing its head. Marsh needed the skeleton to be complete so that he could publish a paper on his find. When a skull was finally found a few miles away from where the skeleton had been discovered, Marsh decided it looked like the right one for such a huge animal. He called the completed skeleton *Brontosaurus*.

In his haste, Marsh made two enormous mistakes. First, he did not realize that he had already discovered a smaller skeleton of this same animal two years earlier and given it a name. He had called it *Apatosaurus*. This new skeleton was so much bigger that he thought it was a different animal altogether, probably a *Brachiosaurus*. Second, the skull Marsh used to complete his *"Brontosaurus"* was from a different kind of dinosaur!

Marsh's error was not discovered at the time, in the way that Cope's head-on-the-tail mistake was. In fact, the correct skull was not put on the skeleton until 1979. That same year, the creature, now finally bearing the correct skull, was rechristened with its original name: *Apatosaurus*. Meanwhile, Marsh's *"Brontosaurus"* had become one of the most popular and best-recognized

In his haste to publish new discoveries, Marsh made the mistake of putting the wrong head on an *Apatosaurus* skeleton. He thought he had discovered a new dinosaur, which he called *Brontosaurus*.

dinosaurs throughout the world. But because Marsh did not carefully compare the bones, it was actually two different dinosaurs combined as one.

In June 1879, Marsh visited the Como Bluff site. Arthur Lakes had traveled there from Colorado to continue digging for Marsh. In August, after Marsh returned home to New Haven, Cope arrived at the site himself. Marsh's team was so worried over Cope's presence that they sent a man to stand in each of the quarries they had dug. They would not let Cope so much as look into any one of them. Lakes himself, after hearing so many terrible things about Cope, finally met him in person. He was surprised to find that he liked the man.

There was now so much suspicion on both sides that no one trusted anyone. Diggers began to make problems among themselves in their own camps. Marsh's group fought with each other constantly. They tracked each other's movements, always suspecting a spy might be among them. Men quit without notice and went to work for a rival team. All the diggers were convinced that others were making better money. No one stayed loyal to his boss for long. Cope and Marsh's jealousy had affected everyone working for them, and finally Lakes decided he'd had enough. He could no longer stand all the bickering. He resigned his position and went home to teach at a school of mining.

Cope and Marsh earnestly desired to leave their mark on the world of paleontology, and they already had, though not necessarily in the way they most wanted. Because of their feud, they would only work against each other. Cooperation was out of the question. That competitive spirit now enveloped almost everyone digging during the great fossil rush at Como Bluff. It was every man for himself. The discoveries at Como Bluff are still considered some of the greatest fossil finds in history, but they might have been even greater if people had been able to trust one another.

10
THE FINAL BATTLE

In the years following the rush on Como Bluff, fortune did not smile on Edward Cope. He was blocked by Marsh from publishing volume two of his life's work on paleontology, and his lack of money also made it impossible to pursue another large-scale fossil-collecting expedition of his own. In addition, his health was often bad, and he probably suffered from malaria, among other illnesses. With his few remaining funds, he invested in a mining company, but the mine failed and Cope lost his money. All Cope had left was his precious and financially valuable fossil collection. He focused his energy on the study of it.

Marsh, on the other hand, was thriving. He received an annual salary of $4,000 in his position as the government survey's chief paleontologist, money that helped him build an expensive mansion near Yale. He never married or had any children, and his expenses were fewer than Cope's. He also commanded the respect and admiration of the academic community. Those who worked for Marsh at Yale's Peabody Museum, however, were not always so impressed. In his state-of-the-art paleontology lab, Marsh was as possessive and jealous of his work as he was in the field with Cope. He forbade his assistants to write or publish anything on the field of vertebrate paleontology. He informed them that they would only be allowed to write about other fields in which Marsh himself did no work.

During this time, Cope had not entirely given up his efforts to have volumes two and

This photograph from the early 1880s was taken on the occasion of Chief Red Cloud's visit to New Haven, Connecticut, where Marsh had made his home. The two had first met in 1874, when Red Cloud permitted Marsh to remove fossils from Sioux lands.

three of his "bible" published. He visited Washington, D.C., to try to convince Congress to put through a bill that would permit them to pay the costs of publishing the books. On several occasions, his request was denied. In 1889, the same year Marsh triumphantly discovered a magnificent horned dinosaur he called *Triceratops*, Cope went back to Washington, D.C., to make the request again. This time, the response was devastating.

Congress still refused to pay for the publication, and this time they delivered additional bad news. They knew that much of Cope's massive fossil collection had been gathered on official government land surveys. The fossils, they claimed, were technically the property of the government. They had decided Cope must hand the fossils over to the Smithsonian National Museum of Natural History in Washington, D.C. The people responsible for making this demand were members of Marsh's old-boy network, influential friends and political allies who always looked out for one another. Cope knew that Marsh was behind this outrageous attempt to strip him of the only thing of value he had left. Marsh was attempting to take his final revenge.

Losing his fossil collection would be the end

of Cope both professionally and personally. He needed to strike back quickly and powerfully. The best way to do this, Cope decided, was to bring his story to the newspapers. In the many years since their feud had begun, Cope had kept a file of all of Marsh's activities, his accusations, and his mistakes. Cope handed over the material to a reporter for the *New York Herald*.

The resulting article was published on January 12, 1890. All of Cope's bitterness, all his suspicions and complaints about Marsh that had been accumulating for decades, were given a voice by the *Herald* reporter. The headline for the article was "Scientists Wage Bitter Warfare." The article attacked both Marsh and the director of the U.S. Geological Survey, John Wesley Powell, who had recommended that the government repossess Cope's fossils. Among other things, the *Herald* article printed Cope's accusations that Marsh had often stolen much of his research from other people and taken credit for it, that he deliberately used his influence with the government to get himself a salaried position as the U.S. Geological Survey's chief paleontologist, and that Marsh's scientific work itself was filled with mistakes.

Until now, most of Cope and Marsh's arguing had appeared in scientific journals, more or less limiting knowledge of their rivalry to the academic community. Now Cope was airing the dirty laundry in the mainstream press for the entire world. The newspapers even printed drawings of Cope and Marsh so people would recognize them. The *Herald* article ended by repeating Cope's assertion that he was only bringing these issues to light because of the threat to take away his fossil collection.

Marsh did not delay in responding. He denied each of Cope's accusations, providing long explanations for every mistake Cope claimed Marsh had made in his work. Then he launched a counterattack of his own accusations against Cope. Back and forth it went in the newspaper for days. Marsh lashed out with his final weapon—the story of Cope's *Elasmosaurus* reconstruction with the head on the end of the tail. Finally, the public grew tired of the bickering, and the paper stopped running the articles. But the damage was done.

By the late 1880s, Cope was in poor health and nearly penniless. However, he fought to keep his fossil collection and to continue his work, as this image of his cluttered study suggests.

Congress was very unhappy with the newspaper stories. The congressmen did not like reading accusations that Marsh had used his friends and allies in the government for his personal gain, and they didn't like attention being brought to how they chose to spend money on geological surveys. Congress decided that the science itself, and all the bad publicity that had come in the wake of the surveys, wasn't worth the money they were spending. They decided to stop funding paleontological work almost entirely. Marsh was told his position of chief paleontologist was being eliminated. He was also told that some of his own fossils that had been collected on government surveys must be turned over to institutions in Washington, D.C.

Cope did win this battle. In the waves of negative publicity, it was quietly decided that he should be allowed to keep his fossil collection. Meanwhile, Marsh lost his position as chief paleontologist and was now being told to hand over some of his fossils. Cope had gotten his revenge. But the cost to the science of paleontology in the loss of government funding was enormous.

The personal attacks printed in the *New York Herald* were the last public conflict between O. C. Marsh and Edward Drinker Cope. The two returned to the work about which they were so passionate. In February 1897, seven years after the *Herald* articles were published, Cope became very ill. He died that April. There is no record of Marsh's reaction to the news.

Two years later, Marsh came down with pneumonia. He died in his home on March 18, 1899. Just a year before the dawn of the twentieth century, two of the founders of the science of paleontology were gone.

O. C. Marsh and Edward Drinker Cope possessed two of the most brilliant minds of nineteenth-century science. Along with Joseph Leidy, they virtually created the field of paleontology. Their discoveries defined the science.

Unfortunately, their bitter rivalry had earned as much space in the history books as their scientific achievements.

Working against each other, Marsh discovered and named eighty-six new species of dinosaurs, and Cope fifty-six. The massive first volume of Cope's "bible" is still considered one of the most important works on paleontology today. Cope's and Marsh's research opened a door to an ancient world unknown to the public—a world of massive, awe-inspiring giants who reigned supreme until their abrupt departure from existence. Lifelong enemies, Cope and Marsh nonetheless wrote the most significant chapter in the history of paleontology during their time together.

It is hard not to wonder what they might have accomplished had they decided to become friends and work together.

EPILOGUE

The great feud between Cope and Marsh is not an isolated event in the history of science. There have been other famous rivalries, such as the relatively recent one between well-known anthropologists Richard and Mary Leakey and Dr. Donald Johanson. Their feud was also over fossilized bones: in this case, the correct age and classification of a skeleton with striking similarities to a human skeleton, but thought to be several million years old. Johanson believed the skeleton, discovered in 1975 and called "Lucy," was of an entirely unknown species, the most ancient common link between our contemporary human line and a second species that had died off. The Leakeys maintained that the evidence was insufficient to support Johanson's theory. The conflict played out unpleasantly with accusations both in print and on television. The resulting bad feelings between the two camps never fully went away. More recent discoveries of even older fossils of human ancestors have not resolved the issue; they have, in fact, created controversies and feuds of their own.

Science is often intensely competitive, and there are several reasons for the rivalries that have existed over the centuries. Scientists are often thought of as wiser than other people, but they are still, first and foremost, imperfect human beings. A scientist passionate enough about his or her work to spend years or decades on research or developing a theory is also someone for whom work may be very personal. Sometimes scientists may not distinguish between themselves and their ideas or theories. They are one and the same. So an attack on the idea is perceived as an attack on the person.

In addition, in many scientific fields, one person's success can mean automatic failure for another. If two artists create paintings at the same time, one will not render the other obsolete. But if a scientist publishes a theory with sound evidence to support the claim, those with similar theories are denied the glory of official credit. They lose the chance to be first. And scientists with opposing theories may then be deemed wrong.

When he was close to completing his work on natural selection that he would publish in *On the Origin of Species,* Charles Darwin received a letter and manuscript from a naturalist named Alfred Wallace, which laid out the very same ideas in extensive detail. Two extraordinary minds, each working independently, produced the same theory of evolution by natural selection at the same time.

If things had played out slightly differently, we might today consider Alfred Wallace to be the father of evolutionary theory. Or Darwin, who had been laboring on his theory for twenty years, might have chosen to go on the offensive. But Darwin did not respond to Wallace by attempting to silence him, discredit him, or eliminate him as competition. Though alarmed to learn that another naturalist had produced an evolutionary theory remarkably similar to his own, he decided the best way to proceed was to make a presentation of his work and Wallace's work simultaneously to the scientific community. The work was presented to the Linnaean Society, a major academic organization devoted to the natural sciences, and Darwin and Wallace were given equal credit in conceiving the theory.

When *Origin of Species* was published in 1859, it was a bestseller, and Charles Darwin became a famous man. Today it is Darwin's name most of us think of when we consider the roots of evolution and natural-selection theory. But it could easily have been Wallace. Or, had Darwin and Wallace become rivals, their names might be linked as Cope's and Marsh's are. Instead, Darwin and Wallace made room for one another and encouraged, rather than discouraged, each other's work. They became colleagues who viewed each other with respect and recognition.

Some scientists will always strive for official credit and academic fame. Others, like Joseph Leidy and Alfred Wallace, are content merely to do brilliant work in historically significant scientific times. Leidy and Wallace may not be household names today, but the academic world remembers them as giants in their fields.

Cope and Marsh called a great deal of attention to themselves with their rivalry, but in the process they helped bring the world of dinosaurs into the public eye. Since then, dinosaurs have remained the star attraction of the world of natural science. In our museums, our movie theaters, and our books, we cannot get enough of them. In the midst of all this attention, new discoveries are constantly being made. In the past ten years, the largest meat-eating dinosaur known to the world was discovered, as well as a tiny flying dinosaur with four wings, and an ancestor of the crocodile measuring roughly the size of a train car. Advances in technology combined with the extraordinary enthusiasm for dinosaur hunting have driven the search for new specimens around the globe. Paleontologists are not only discovering new dinosaurs, they are rethinking accepted notions about known species. *T. rex*, for example, may not have been the Godzilla-like savage predator we have imagined. At least one scientist believes *T. rex* may have been a slow, lumbering creature who scavenged the kills of other dinosaurs rather than hunting and killing for itself. Other research seems to show that *T. rex* might have had feathers.

The human elements of jealousy and pride fueled the bitter rivalry between Cope and Marsh. But other human elements, such as intellectual curiosity and passion, ensure that the hunt for dinosaurs will endure. Now more than ever, new discoveries are being made at an astonishing rate. In the century that has passed since Cope and Marsh opened the door to dinosaur hunting, the field has grown enormously. There is room for every aspiring paleontologist, and much left over to spare. At this very moment, there are countless active digs going on throughout the world.

The next spectacular find could well happen tomorrow.

BIBLIOGRAPHY

Ackroyd, Peter. *Voyages Through Time: The Beginning.* New York: DK Publishing, Inc., 2003.

Colbert, Edwin H. *Men and Dinosaurs: The Search in Field and Laboratory: The Great Dinosaur Hunters and Their Discovery of the World of the Prehistoric Reptiles.* New York: E. P. Dutton & Co., Inc., 1968.

Dinosaur Encyclopedia: From Dinosaurs to the Dawn of Man. New York: DK Publishing, Inc., and American Museum of Natural History, 2001.

Gayrard-Valy, Yvette. *Fossils: Evidence of Vanished Worlds.* New York: Harry N. Abrams, Inc., 1994.

Hellman, Hal. *Great Feuds in Science: Ten of the Liveliest Disputes Ever.* New York: John Wiley & Sons, Inc., 1998.

Holmes, Thom. *Fossil Feud: The Rivalry of the First American Dinosaur Hunters.* New Jersey: Julian Messner, 1997.

Howard, Robert West. *The Dawnseekers: The First History of American Paleontology.* New York: Harcourt Brace Jovanovich, Inc., 1975.

Jaffe, Mark. *The Gilded Dinosaur: The Fossil War Between E. D. Cope and O. C. Marsh and the Rise of American Science.* New York: Crown, 2000.

Kohl, Michael F., and John S. McIntosh, editors. *Discovering Dinosaurs in the Old West: The Field Journals of Arthur Lakes.* Washington and London: The Smithsonian Institution Press, 1997.

Lanham, Url. *The Bone Hunters: The Heroic Age of Paleontology in the American West.* New York: Dover Publications, Inc., 1992.

Wallace, David Rains. *The Bonehunters' Revenge: Dinosaurs, Greed, and the Greatest Scientific Feud of the Gilded Age.* Boston and New York: Houghton Mifflin Company, 1999.

PICTURE CREDITS

Photos courtesy of:

American Museum of Natural History Library (pp. 8, 21, 26, 35, 59, 67, 70, 85, 99).

Ewell Sale Stewart Library, The Academy of Natural Sciences of Philadelphia (pp. iii, 22, 31, 36–37).

Library of Congress, Washington, D.C., U.S.A. (pp. 11, 19, 43, 46).

Linda Hall Library of Science, Engineering & Technology (pp. 78–79).

Peabody Museum of Natural History, Yale University, New Haven, Connecticut, U.S.A. (pp. 16, 49, 74, 80, 90–91, 95).

INDEX

113

ABOUT THE AUTHOR

 ELIZABETH CODY KIMMEL is the author of several novels and nonfiction books for early and middle-grade readers, including *Ice Story: Shackleton's Lost Expedition, As Far As the Eye Can Reach: Lewis and Clark's Westward Quest, Before Columbus: The Leif Eriksson Expedition,* and *Balto and the Great Race,* which won the Kansas City Children's Book Award for grades 1 to 3.

Ms. Kimmel lives in the Hudson Valley in New York with her husband and daughter.